Finding God on Mayberry Street

Finding God on Mayberry Street

Seasons of Spirituality in Poems and Reflections

Beauty, Donna

REVEREND DONNA
MINISTRIES

Omaha, Nebraska

Please seek the counsel of a professional if you need assistance with a mental illness or medical need. This book is not intended to be a replacement for professional consultation.

Photos used on the cover and throughout the book are from the personal collection of Donna Knutson.

Reverend Donna's books are available to order from your favorite bookseller or from Amazon.com.

All Scripture quotations, unless otherwise indicated, are taken from The New International (NIV) Bible.

Reverend Donna Ministries

c/o CMI

4822 South 133rd Street

Omaha, NE 68137

Color Paperback ISBN: 978-0-9997488-1-7

Black & White Paperback ISBN: 978-0-9997488-4-8

Mobi ISBN: 978-0-9997488-2-4

EPUB ISBN: 978-0-9997488-3-1

Library of Congress Cataloging Number: 2017919348

Printed in the USA

10 9 8 7 6 5 4 3 2

To whom I love with deep gratitude:
My Husband, Paul—my love, my support and companion
forever in my heart—my children:
Joshua and Caitlin, Brian, Kate and Hannah
Margaret and Taylor
The Tinies:
Broin, Houston and Ivory

Friends who knew I needed food for the body,
as well as food for the soul:
Joan Field
Beth Ashley-Carnes
Sharon Boynton
Loyie Weber

Friends who prayed for me and believed in the power
of transformation and the call:
Rev. Dr. Eric Elnes
Rev. Dr. Chris Alexander
And the many friends of:
Countryside Community Church, United Church of Christ, Omaha, NE
One Spirit Interfaith Seminary, NYC

Introduction

Writing *Finding God on Mayberry Street* is really about finding my voice as I journeyed through becoming an Interfaith Minister in the middle years of my life. I wrote daily as a spiritual practice, noticing the beauty within people, nature, family, and my faith communities. Whether that be my seminary home in New York City, or looking out my sunroom windows at my little yellow cottage, I am experiencing the revelation that is before me in any given moment.

Take a moment to pause and enjoy the beauty.

Beauty, Donna

Summer

Sometimes it takes a whole lot of people to lay their hands on you

To bless you,

to lift you up,

to hold your truth before your face,

and to sing Alleluias into your ear.

It takes women who come through the front door,

who cradle the Light

in deep wells of hope and gratitude for who you were born to be.

And who

you have fought to become.

It takes edge walkers

who know how to burn

through the veil—

though bitter for a short while—

until the fragrance of rose petals

fills the dimly lit,

firmly formed,

the impossible vision

you chose to dream

while walking deeply into the woods

searching for roots…

hoping for water jugs to pour over

heads

hands

feet.

Making mystery as you breathe

Beauty, Donna

Oh, the people you know and the places you'll go.

Someone says, "You're an introvert?" and I smile, leaning rarely into labels of fashion anymore

and I love mystics and the madness

that some call

"the Great Unknown."

But I smile and meditate,

sending rays off my fingertips to the one who seems a bit more veiled,

the one who has forgotten the wisdom in a Sabbath rest that

shifts shapes in the clouds,

shifts shapes in thoughts floating by.

I begin to hear Teresa of Avila wandering out back near the pergola and we read pages of "Thunder Perfect Mind"* and share a thin package of lemon cookies and green tea.

Someone says, "You're a religious nut?" or "are you more along the lines of spiritual?"

…and the words barely catch.

I've been free for so long…and the fruit from the tree begins to fall and the Japanese Maple blazes a burnt red…

Honey flows from the landscape of kingdoms and peace…

Silk worms throw threads that entangle my thoughts and dreams,

and for days I watch the netting form,

while poetry is read aloud in the gardens…

And the dogs listen,

along with the birds of the air.

We hear music up the hill from the man who lost his son a few weeks ago, and the neighborhood softens around the ash trees they are removing from across the street from his home. They are old and diseased; and the man lost his son. The trees are coming down, and the man now sees empty land.

For a few moments, Christ is walking in the garden,

and the Buddha sits on the curb.

The trash men go by and their truck rumbles on.

*The Nag Hammadi Scriptures

Nothing is disturbed

yet

everything changes.

I find more poets to join me in the garden.

They hold images.

They marry words with peace and

find places for commas and periods.

They live

down

deep.

They ask me different questions

like—

"Do you feel the way the words pray?"

Beauty, Donna

This is the Age

Rising from dirt takes energy; failing takes nothing at all.

Bending thoughts to the beat of hummingbird wings

Requires standing still, patience nurturing the heavy tide, and cleansing the palette from ordinary to holy delight. Wash away…and return… wash away, and return.

Holding words as sacred messengers, handing over pain to angels watching from the corners of a room. Knowing, and knowing, and knowing we are heard, we are form, we are temple in a time.

Filtering actions, finding grace, fracturing flip charts. Falling in love with sacred space, spirit's breath, songs of nature, the waves in the grass.

Digging through layers of human frailty takes compassion, requires might. Finding bigger words for empathy. Erasing harsh white chalk lines from vocabularies. Softening the resistance to something that is "our own".

Too many words from a book and we are lost for days. Someone else's home, someone else's healing that wraps its arms around our soul. Pulling us in, pulling apart phrases that involve not one life, but many. It's so easy to live alone. To watch, to wonder, to see and then to close the door.

But Holy asks the impossible, replaces the lonely, captures the dream, erases nothing. Holy claims the healed, receives the wholeness, paints colors on faces of the forgotten, waves in, nods to, calls forth… waits for, turns away no one. Remembers it all.

The evolving that grows us up, way past forests and trees. Way past third grade dreams and aspirations from our twenties. The beyond, the beyond that threads the story to the cause. The realms to the glory. The lover, to the heart.

Beauty, Donna

The first day of summer arrived with the humming silence of prayer. It came before my eyes opened. Such a conversation given from within and a strawberry moon. Spirit whispering gifts that only human ears can hear after years of penetrating borders and deepening roots. For there is no other heaven, only the one we create as magnolia and wisteria. That dream state of here and beyond, mingling with the smell of ripe peaches and a three-year-old black lab.

Holy happenings in the world, right now. Holy happenings that disrupt and tangle us up in the divine language of activism. The force of deep witnessing and standing straight, instead of off to the side while others tend to life.

We are the people, called and ignited with correcting and collaborating. Perhaps a colossal task, but I see much further. And I want it to be while I still breathe, while the mail carrier drops off letters on Mayberry Street and while my grandson grows healthy and strong in his mama's tummy.

Ramblings on a Monday in June, before the cottage door opens to the neighborhood and the peace of the Lord passes out on the street and we are amongst the people.

Beauty, Donna

In my younger years I called her Thirst.

She followed me everywhere until my babies were grown until there were no more days where I could, wait…

For Thirst, knew I'd long for the rest of my days

wandering through taverns, along dry Autumn pathways…past the old barn

where new kittens had been born, drenched in birth…

She knew that being born was what happens when your Spirit is not small, but on fire…

That to look in the mirror and see Light, was to experience pain, to crack like the section of fence I balanced on as a child…waiting to fall through…knowing I would tumble onto…tumble beyond…waving to mysteries that come with the Thirst…pardoned by nothing…curious about movements that were shadows that held presence and soul…

Thirst found me in my fifties…and took pity on my longing…She found a tiny pump beyond the shed near the pergola…where the trumpet vines go wild in July…where something cool would splash onto my hands… into my bones…

Every day she would introduce me to something of Glory…the crown blush of a rose…and my Thirst gave way to a ringing, then a song…a little mantra that passed through my lips as I bowed to the earth, as I bowed to the spring that had begun to tickle at the back of my throat… the rattling within my heart… space for a reunion with the baptism of rivers…to reach for the glass off the counter that seemed too small, when the stream within me seemed to flow from a depth that I had only encountered as a child, walking the fields, rolling in dirt…playing with my children…in those early years, Thirst had just begun to nudge me towards the sea…

Beauty, Donna

What has married you to the world? So many of us take vows. We recite words of blessings and benedictions, whether we hear them as holy language or not.

We look to the outer world for recognition that we have accomplished the task and yet, the entirety of our lives are lived from the inside out.

What has married you to the world? When I said yes to ministry, to God, I took vows.

Spirit wrestled the deepest, darkest parts of my inner landscape and scraped and tore away layers and layers of crusted-over piles of history and stories…And I say stories, because they can truly accumulate over the years as far less about truth, as perhaps wounded visions and failures.

When I look outwards now, my vows are richer and clearer than they ever have been. What work there is before us requires so much courage. A voice of strength and passion that comes from the inner life.

When I started seminary, I knew it would be a huge step in cultivating and nourishing voice for this time in my life. That awakening is so much more than the mystical. It is everything, when combined with the intimate and vulnerable opening to the beauty and magnificence of what is trying to expand for us, within us and through us. Spirit is speaking and moving through people. I have never heard such a clattering and a shouting from the realms as now.

We are here for a reason. It is not a joke or an illusion. God enters in day in and day out, over and over again. We are the conversations and the bearers of the Light.

Beauty, Donna

I planted a lot of tulips and purple allium last fall in the gardens,

Eighty-two bulbs, to be exact.

And when I came home from a long trip to the concrete city,

I counted them ceremoniously,

While feeling into the violets and yellows,

While bending low to inspect their soft edges and the beauty of their folds.

I counted with a number in my head, as perhaps some bulbs could not push their way through the cracks in the earth, the way life gets a bit solid, or stagnant, or just downright saturated with too much

thought.

And I wanted to know, and I wanted to survive.

The spring had been rainy, with cold winds; an April of dark skies.

Nights where the fireplace was on

well past eight and I wore bedroom slippers on the wooden floors.

The dogs didn't seem to realize that the earth had softened; and we could sit out longer in the evenings if we wished.

But we stayed in, reading books until the sunset rested on the neighbor's pines.

And then, if I could find the right weight of coat, and the dogs didn't pull too harshly on the leashes,

We would walk the park for half an hour,

And come back to the cottage, for something warm, like a cup of peach tea with a tiny slice of

strawberry pie, from the restaurant, leftovers from a lunch with a friend.

I counted seventy-eight tulips, while slipping a purple shawl over my shoulders;

Talking to the dogs, picking branches off the ground from the storm

that awakened me at three that morning.

Seventy-eight is a good number, and I'm beginning to see summer.

Beauty, Donna

Finding God on Mayberry Street

Summertime has its own holy sky,

Rain in the mountains, drips touching the sea.

Splashes in the Carolinas and dry land in Tulsa.

Summertime of my sorrow,

Where business is real,

How nothing is ordinary.

Schedules turned into something of the past.

And what do I do with my days?

I watch the holy sky move in the clouds.

Canadian geese shoot up off the lake

I listen, just listen.

Waiting for the ordinary to return.

For God to correct something that is missing in me.

For sorrow to be presented in words on a page.

For heaven and earth to cause a rumble,

Deep down in the interior, with a sound, or a voice that I recognize as one who is wiser and knows of these things.

In the breaking of my soul, in the quieting of the mind.

For the arch of a rainbow to offer prayers up in my name.

God will hear, so God will send a cure,

And this time will pass.

Summertime of my sorrow

Grateful for the past

Memories, and how love can turn an ordinary holy sky

Into sun showers and green grass. I must now mow.

Beauty, Donna

I said one of my dangerous prayers. You know, one of the ones that change your life. The ones you can't live without. Whispering through the heart just before six and the dawn.

Cardinals just beginning their chatter in the weeping mulberry outside my bedroom window. Catching sight of a red wing before the blind is fully opened.

Prayers once uttered, are gone…and that exciting fear and trembling greeting me in the middle of my gut.

How will it appear this time?

The desires of my heart. The way Spirit meets matter, trees leaning towards light,

children growing up and away.

We are given second and third chances at life; we are given life.

No one seems surprised anymore that God is in nature,

That spells can be broken; and people are healed.

That we are battling for freedom; that snowdrops bloom the day we have leap year.

We have grown steady in what we see as pushing through obstacles,

finding the rose amidst the thorns,

moving our feet into Mystery.

Praying dangerous prayers that are answered in perfect timing,

experiencing Light as normal and every day.

Humble acceptance,

bent in the middle while radiant and strong.

Hard not to believe the veil is thinning, the stories are radical,

like Pentecost and the fiery consuming.

Hearing Spirit in our own tongues.

Something soothing about power that knows its own body through awakening.

That hears from beyond while present.

That contains the Source, while walking the ordinary and praying dangerous prayers.

Beauty, Donna

The summer is easy on Mayberry Street.
The orange tabby cat taunts my year-old Cooper,
and tiny ones play with Play-Doh on hot afternoons.
The heavy push is over now,
and though miracles are stirring inside the cave,
empty is good for another few days.
Praying is sweeping the kitchen floor
and the nightly watering of zinnias and pink coneflowers.
Praying is comfortable as the mind takes a rest
and the body seeks the sand and water.

Beauty, Donna

It rained today
and I talked about Jesus.
It's been a long-time dream to do just that…
that's why I bought a robe and a stole…
It's why Spirit moved from the inside to the outside,
why the sky blends often with the flowers
and back to the realms of in-between and diseases of the mind.
It's why exhaustion has disappeared; and this tranquil bliss of happiness
radiates throughout me…
Decades come, and decades go
and fifties drew the lines and erased the boundaries.
Sixty was the enunciation and emancipation
where death just wanders in and through
laughing at the stories that dissolve.
And I learned to smile from a different place in my body—
to open pockets that freed the space
To defeat the fog
to burn through and alongside
the short amount of days
one is given on earth.
How wisdom knows and we can truly decide when we will
know too…
It rained today
and I talked about Jesus
as poetry and parables sound the same to me
as Psalms and singing
release worship that no one else can see.
It rained today
and I talked about Jesus…
And I fell in love
once more.

Beauty, Donna

And still life goes on.

"Bearing fruit in every good work." (Col. 1:10)

The lake is higher than normal this year,

The lawn needs to be mowed more often than just on a Saturday morning

Before six, when people are dreaming with their windows open;

And the sound of a motor engaging with the pull of the lever

Sets the day of chores into motion.

And still life goes on…

When something has changed, or the dog wishes to have a rest in the peony bushes,

the vases then filled with soft pinks and heavy heads of abandonment, once wild.

"Bearing fruit in every good work." (Col. 1:10)

I rinse the glasses set down in the sink from the night before,

And place them in the drainer,

memories of the night before,

And bowls of salsa and chips in the wicker basket out on the patio.

Summer evening with a friend…talking about, feeling into, inquiring tilts of the head; holding sacred

space for what comes from the heart as the sun sets beyond the fence line and we say our goodbyes for

another year.

Why is it we see far away friends just once a year?

And a myriad of responses began to come to the surface.

In the morning I will slide the kayak onto the water.

In the morning is my Sabbath rest, when all the chores are done.

The water smooth, the dishes stacked back onto the shelf.

And still life goes on…

Beauty, Donna

And we shall lift each other up,
higher and higher…
a cup of peach tea
in the morning hour of prayer
while the gardens search
and roots thirst
for the holy threads
of healing eyes
and flashes of birth.
And we shall lift each other up,
higher and higher
in the heat,
in the season of betwixt and between
before we know who we have become
and to what we have been transformed,
and to how less has created our freedom.
Morning musings…
from the beginning to the end
and across the horizon
where the cross unites
and we can sing
Glory Hallelujah.
So, roll back the stone
or walk near the shore.
Collect your disciples
of every color
and every faith
of every elder born.

Tell of grace.

Warn of hope.

Make new.

Bring peace…

There is a cup for everyone.

Beauty, Donna

It's amazing how many breaths we take in a day and how many breaths we hold onto until we know life is all right again. Whether we remember to celebrate life or not…whether the surprises come into our lives as joys or sorrows…deepening the breath, the longing to hold onto friends and family.

I don't think life is so much about nail biting as it is holding onto the heart of another.

We ask for peace while the chaos spins around us.

We rest in the love of others who are stronger and perhaps braver in moments when we are the weakest.

But together we celebrate life, the hurdles, the frantic avenues of discovering who we are in such moments.

And we lean inwards on Grace, remembering that we are here for moments in a splash of eternity and we breathe through life's awakenings.

Beauty, Donna

Why must there be seven gods or seventy, when I know only One?

Who designed a sky in seven continents, with oceans near the shore?

Who named the God of the Abrahamic faiths or the Hindu Lords,

The Great Spirit sitting in a circle around the fire?

The Divine Feminine opening as birth unto the world.

The earth filled with intelligence and worth.

Tongues spoken in many languages, dialects with disturbances.

Wisdom written, children holding thread by thread, country by country,

Boat load, ship wrecked, grasslands that were empty before we were born.

Worship that happened, altars no higher than a single rock with communion and community.

With heart, with soul.

Mystics and seers, the Way Showers,

Dreamers, fallen out fallen onto, fallen open.

Light that can only expand, transform, reveal.

There has been a Pentecost in every color and every nation.

More than red, yellow or orange. Those added tastes of spices and wines.

Frankincense and Myrrh. Lavender grown in organic fields and tied with pure white ribbons and placed in mailing packages for those waiting vigil with their mothers.

Beauty that does not speak to yours or just mine.

Five hundred creation stories.

Pillars of suffering and angels of the night,

Wandering, blinded, awakened, divine messengers, spirit guides, desert fathers and mothers,

Fire walkers, priests and all the stoles of ordination and lay ministers

And for all those called to…Life.

Beauty, Donna

nd she asked me, "So, how is it that God is so very real to you?"

The word imagination immediately springs to mind, as well as John O'Donohue and his flavor of life so similar to my own. There are thousands of people living as wonder makers and real-life Spirit bodies. I find light in their eyes and hope in their hugs. They are willing to angle their bodies close to those whispering death notices or pains in the heart. They reveal a God of light, found in the dark times.

They are pinpointed with tiny flags on the visual world map of my heart, and I can reach out to them, sending poetry and wisdom quotes, and they wink back at me across the miles.

I AM here…I AM here.

I had a dear friend who passed on a few years back. She sent tiny vials of tears in a bottle after she had lost a child and asked me to bless them and send them back to her. God manifested in physical form. Take those tears and breathe into them. Bless the hours she took to gather them off her cheeks, slipping to the bottom of her face and dropping into the vial.

"You must become like a child again", and find ways to bear witness to the mystical awakening and discipline that Spirit requires. Offer up, give into, pick the hardest challenge, acknowledge that all things are made new. Create from the ashes, wade in the waters. Balance the sweetness with the salt…find honey-making bees.

Tearing things out and planting new seeds. Restoring the laughter bubbles that Spirit brings to the surface and the fiery rain that keeps the heart open after suffering for and with others.

Switching thought patterns and riding the waves…

Finding kingdoms within that are far more real than the disturbances in the atmosphere. Or find the people who have just forgotten how to live with a holy light weaving through their cells…Breathing for them and with them…Lining tiny tissue paper flowers in the garden, because I believe they too will grow…Dropping seeds of imagination….Grateful for the gift of the child restored, and drawing freely outside of the lines…Now, turn the page…

Beauty, Donna

So, at the end of the day, some things were simple and easy to hear of God; other things went whisking by and I wondered why?

The weeds were so easy to pull after the rain. And mums slid easily into the ground with a gentle tap of a foot around their roots—holding them firm to the earth.

Sending so many prayers out on the breath:

—for friends and their parents; for friends and their children;

—for women to be rescued and babies to thrive; for illness to pass gently from the body and hope to rescue the heart when it is fading.

—for monsters to come out from under the bed; for mothers to rest in their daughter's care; for souls to be heard and bees to be holy.

There's sun in the sky and the darkness at night. What's hard can be a gift and what's remembered can be the promise.

Rainbows still hold covenant and weddings give us vows.

Hope and mercy, grace and peace, beauty and death, song and vibration. Holy on a day in September, where we learn width and height. We hear blue jays squawking and squirrels running the wires.

There are those who look into the abyss and those who do not. Some things will always remain and some things will pass.

Spirit moves…holding the restless, releasing the eternal sigh, relaxing into, between and through. Angels work and kingdoms are built, sweetness and darkness, mixed.

Beauty, Donna

Spirit never ignores a broken heart or the madness of a dream that allows us to create a new life.

Spirit never ignores anything that gives us space to expand into the blossoms on a magnolia tree, or look at the way cattle settle into peaceful rest in the evening hours. The colors that pierce the darkness, just seconds before dawn. The synchronicity of hearing something over and over again, until you truly listen to the message and the voice of God.

The way humans rise up at just the right moment of Spirit pressing deep and with strength, into the heart of the world. The pressure of a hand directly on the heart within the chest to make a choice, a decision to walk further, a chance to make something right or to hear authentic and personal truth.

There are many awakening moments for people; and there is much sleep in the world. On the days when the sky is gray, there is more resistance. On the afternoons of sipping tea and sunlight pouring through the sunroom, a hospital window, or the crack in a bedroom blind, there are opportunities for remembering to whom we belong.

There is a wisdom that knows how to create beauty and harmony; how to fight diseases of the heart, mind, body and soul. There is a wisdom to drag us out of despair and blindness, into the eternity of the everyday dragons and the mystery of miracles and mayhem.

The edge is a place of great compassion for souls who travel deep and travel far. The edge is a different kind of journey than most but worth the battles and the dragons we slay along the way. Worth the amount of drowning to reach the shore and the peace that passes all understanding.

Beauty, Donna

I have only known this God of grace and mercy.

This God of transformation and adoration.

The God who I pray to and worship, who I sing to and create story from.
And tonight, all I desire and all that I am is prayer…

Because of You, I pray

and more often than not,

there are no words or beautiful phrases coming off my lips.

Because of You, I pray

and the world changes…as we breathe a common sigh

that I never can write, nor speak, nor share in a crowd.

Because of You, I pray

and all the vows and promises we have made together

spiral up and down the columns of my spine.

God incarnate…God of healing sorrows this night.

God of messengers and those who will not run and hide.

Because of You, I pray

and you rise up, like the heat off the New York City streets,

off the rain-drenched Nebraska fields,

back home in a tiny farm house where a family gathers,

walking down aisles with stoles around necks and hearts filled with fire.

Because of You, I pray

and the world is magnetic…

a constant, a delight,

nothing rehearsed or held back

or unforgiven…

Because of You, I pray

and there are miracles that supply

and sanctuary in the soul…

There is disciple and sorting through…emptiness…

calm centers and sacred rests…

Because of You, I pray

and fall in love with my enemies,
lie down in the breezes,
fashion hollyhock dolls
with soft pink dresses and heads that nod.
Because of You, I pray
and nothing gets in the way
of loving You.

Beauty, Donna

Yes, all kinds of prayers…
I say them for everyone:

for those messaging with hearts and tears,

for those across seas and around the corner of Mayberry Street,

for those who are upset at the grocery store or for the child who scraped her knee,

for the ones who are in hospital beds and for mothers who are tired of questioning two-year-olds,

for friends who are separated and friends who are sitting on patio chairs planning retirement vacations,

prayers for newlyweds and babies being born,

for those standing next to graveyards and those

braiding their grandchildren's hair.

I heard there were prayers written but I needed to say my own,

for God is closest in my heart

when we are praying alone;

they seem so very tiny, but they mean so very much

to those who ask for kindness, and those who forget the rules,

for the ones who need the blessing,

and the ones who ask for strength

the prayer has already been said,

and the love is already given.

Beauty, Donna

Some of my most ordinary days are blessed by the Flame.

A simple stop at a diner and the glow radiates as the woman in the apron drops off a bowl of hot chicken noodle soup and a croissant.

She does not know the blessing that tapped her gently on the shoulder as she returns to the next guest. But words spill from beyond creating a shield, the gossamer lining meant for spirits and angels working next to God…and the Light gently quiets and moves on.

How many more stops before I am home?

The dry cleaner lady says she is going to see her son tonight in the hospital, he is doing better…and the Light shimmers off her thin cotton blouse as she goes to the back of the shop to reach high into the racks to pull out my order. There is a faint melody that I hear from this song about there being hope in the morning and hope at noon. And I am reminded that hope is not an emotion…but what happens after the struggle.

There are more standing on the corners now. Every year the major intersections hold thin bodies on concrete dividers, where cars go by, hundreds and thousands by the end of the day. The red change purse next to me and the young man who approaches the car. I didn't know he would be the one, the intuitive nudge pressing against my heart. Listen now before he's gone and Spirit moves lightly where there is work to be done. Light resting now on his arm as he reaches to the door to take the money from my hand. His eyes are lit with a dull spit that could have blown out something within me if I had stayed too long, but just for a second he touched the tip of my fingers and the spark hit the both of us and his eyes were not lonely in his aloneness.

I arrive just ten minutes later to the cottage, driving up on the red cobblestones where I park my car. Neighbors mowing yards, dogs walking their companions in the streets as the sidewalks don't start for a few blocks past the park and the college. There are mailboxes we walk out to, waving at people raking leaves in October, strollers passing to find the swings and the slide.

I carry these messages back and forth...Sometimes the rays dance a bit to the side of my vision and for seconds the realms collide and the remembering is like the beginning of a dream I had last night...and when I woke Spirit was praying within me, and the reality of a new day is that it is the first day of my life and revelation is about to happen... hour by hour...

Passing messages from beyond...

Beauty, Donna

Fall

It's three in the morning.
   The ancestors have all passed over,
prayers have risen,
Trick or Treaters are snug in their beds
and for the most part I know where my children are in the world, and
that is comforting.
Pajamas have switched to flannel.
Extra blankets are on the bed.
An occasional turn of the thermostat to one degree warmer
and November is here with golden shouts from the trees
and bags of leaves on the curb for the morning.
I know far less now about anything
for certain
than when I begin to follow Spirit
in and through
around the corner
beyond the climbing roses
and off in the distance.
Following towards
the injustices,
the songs that I sing
the strength that I feel
the mercy that is there
the faith that moves mountains
the community that continues to climb
the family of hope that rises up…
And yet, it is so different…this traveling as one
amongst the many
this listening so deeply that I break often
from the tenderness
and the branches I step over in the woods;

or the direction I will take at the top of the hill.

The slip of the foot

the nod of the head

the acceptance of God around me

breathing deeply through my lungs.

I have just begun to find the beauty of a new day

—how to orchestrate a sound I've been following for a long time—

for no time,

and for all of eternity—

and in decades to come

years that are left to marvel at,

days with mirrors and holy images of chalices of love.

It happens every time

this stretching of the atmosphere

as seasons change

less is known.

Wandering leads to discovery

settling in

yawning at four a.m.

The thinning…of the veil.

Beauty, Donna

Sunday Seminary Stories:

I fly home, window seat, airplane cold, wearing my daughter's boots, a pleasing loan of comfort from home. Exit row and the question from the flight attendant, "Will you be able to assist in case there is a need?" We all answer "yes" and I turn towards the dark out the window. My thoughts of the weekend in New York City and One Spirit. There is no other way for me to be as present in the world, other than in ministry to the Christ…Some say another name, another form or some feeling that they have been touched by a hidden God moving through the eithers. But, it doesn't really matter how, it just matters.

There is a man sitting next to me, playing games on his phone; and the flight attendant is sweet, with short wavy blonde hair, probably around my age. She smiles a lot. Warm heart. Present with people.

We did deep soul work over the weekend. I close my eyes, folding my hands and leaning my chin there to rest. One elbow on the arm rest and the other on my teal pillow on my lap.

God of my heart.

God of my knowing.

Spirit of ever present reality and transformation.

Time is gone, for how long, I do not know and then I hear this little whisper close to my left ear, "Are you praying?"

And I turn to see the man so very close to me, looking me in the eyes. And I laugh and come up from the stillness and say quietly, "Yes, I am." He sits back in his chair for nearly a whole three seconds before going further into the invitation.

So, every minister at one time or a thousand times will deal with the question "So if you pray to this God of Love, then why is the world this way?" But the man with the whisper to his voice didn't go in that direction. He was curious and wanted to ask me questions about the seminary I go to and why the direction of Interfaith. Why become a minister?

We talked about peace that centers at the heart; the focus that it takes to be passionate about relationships and the world. We mirrored back to one another. In my head I called him Phil, though we never exchanged names, just the eye and the heart.

I followed Phil out of the plane two hours later and when we were just about to turn our separate directions, he touched my arm and said, "Thank you for praying and for talking to me and sharing what I want to believe is true in the world."

I smiled all the way to the baggage claim area and part of me knew that God just said, "Gotcha!" And the fire burns and the glory reigns…

Beauty, Donna

ost of life begins with a whisper… a sigh that slips through the unconscious mind, the bridge between human and divine…raising the bar…giving us jiggle room to live a different kind of life…there are no notes any more. Nothing more than thin layers dividing land from the sea, a clear lane that resides between ethereal sound and make believe. Peter Pan, a ship in the sky, a way to live enchanted, before the mystery flies over…beyond the eye…and heaven looks like…feels like…sounds like…smells like…a way through where nothing is divided.

Breathing God takes concentration, purity runs like…peach juice down the chin, laughter from a child, finding honey on the tongue as ordinary…dressing in robes no one can see, and purple, drapes nicely in the heat of the day. Some will say it is only play, and a new day begins with thin sheets of the invisible…wide roads of possible, milky white and radiant. Stepping into, standing beside, claiming victory, ignoring nothing other than the speed in which you die. Born for this…

To be alchemy and dreamer all at the same time…tantalized by burning through layers while walking the streets catching whiffs of perfume… Julian of Norwich no further down the road than a few hundred years. And I can still hear her saying…"this God of yours walks in mysterious ways, I've heard it too…." And the sunrise begins to taint the Nebraska sky…a slight puff of cloud coverage begins on the edge, a yellow hue… Prayers slip through the heart space, between kingdoms of glory and powers of might…I call on all the guidance that waits nearby…and another holy day begins. The world within the world.

Beauty, Donna

ife continues to surprise and amuse! Mayberry Street is abundant with college students, retirees, dog walkers and the neighbor who plays jazz for endless hours on a Sunday afternoon.

Mayberry Street became the place of transition, when we sold our big house on 84th street and my hubby and I began the new life of commuting between states and across boundaries. It's the home that downsized one of us, and centered the road of a contemplative.

What was, is no longer…and shedding was not only necessary, but desired from a deep spirituality. The God who intervened and cleared the tables. The God who knew a deliberate way of freeing the slaves. The God who disrupted and married a queen in disguise.

The little yellow cottage became the sought-after calm in a long period of storms. A harbor to rest and renew. The ground that only I could break through. Fortitude would become the spine and backbone. A steadfastness that required complete clearing in order to become visible.

Beauty, Donna

It's kind of a frenzy until you still, you stop.

You don't need anything anymore.

The seeking is over, the breath work is done.

Morning rises, regardless of imperfections and lapses.

Worship happens, even when you don't, or you think you can't, but you do.

Love melts through the core long before you are born.

Layers burn off.

Some get lost in fables and stories, then stop and find their place.

Some just keep walking, touching, bowing.

Healing, sensing, resting, and kneeling.

Worship happens even when you don't, or you think you can't, but you do.

When you are not just body, or form caught in a lie.

Worship flows into and through, despite and because.

When you are not bird from the sky, or names from the past.

Why you could be, Breath, of the One.

Beauty, Donna

For so long I was so small…forgetting to bless, to brighten, to bemoan what was outside the front door. I was young, not wise…busy, not present. But awakening has its ups and downs, it's radical turn of the door handle and walking towards the sky, the neighborhood, the grocery store. Awakening knows how to inside out, right-side up, a backwards analysis of what is heavenly, what is reality…

For so long I was so small…I heard the sounds but the voice was unsure…lacking, weak…Unable to connect to the passion, the magnetic line towing me closer and closer to realms of glory and that Voice… oh, that Voice…She is Mine…She is strong and clear…She is noble and worthy…She is defined by her center, the constant design of her breath. The way she lingers for seconds in the pause, adjusting to the rhythm of Spirit's light…Waiting for the words to descend into the body…to touch bone before speaking…and now it's been years…I hear her day in and day out…The way she calms and soothes the crowd, the tone, the constant wave of wonder that sweeps through her…She is older and holds court in the interior rooms and corridors…She wades deeper into the drought…She carries water to the thirsty…She stands on the land of the Holy…Voice

Beauty, Donna

For the longest day and night, the shortest month and year, life just knelt beside me, waiting.

I studied words, raised babies as fresh root from the womb of time.

Carried bags of mulch in my arms, crawling through muddied field without form

just to heal; to manage; to find a space with a tunnel that had the tube of a bulb.

And there I slid...to the ground...to the emptiness where Holy had no form or features.

But there was sound...

For the longest day and night, the shortest month and year, life just knelt beside me, waiting.

I studied words, raised babies as fresh root from the womb of time.

I carried a hundred voices that knew languages in forms of every generation, culture and faith.

I held within me, stories of every woman and child, grandparent, teacher.

And I whispered so much off into the distance, that was heard.

I sheltered nothing from Light, and saw only the nearest edge of the Darkness.

Beauty, Donna

How did we get so far from Narnia, and walking, and kneeling at curbs before crossing into thresholds?

Before opening to portals we thought were just stories that other people live, that only others could write into their lives?

Hannah and I have been cleaning out my library. Stacks of books that will go up into the attic space, and others, the favorites, the ones I can't physically be away from, the covers that I recognize as gold—

The pages tagged with yellow, green and blue tabs on almost every other page.

Those piles go ceremoniously back onto the shelves, and although they are organized in categories, like spiritual writers, poets, and mystics. The style of writing is not so much what divides my attention, but what I've heard within me as the years go by.

Narnia coming closer and closer to heaven on earth. To the realms of Glory that I've witnessed as healing and conscious expansiveness. To the heroes and those fallen on swords of the past and the heroes of the present, who put it all out there on paper with black ink. The heroes who are vulnerable and raw because they live the call of our time. To be present to the one life within you. To be awake enough to see a bit of an angel standing next to a friend who is dying; to be conscious enough to stop talking when it's just gibberish you've practiced for too long; to be quiet within you. That your interior body expands and you don't know how…You don't even question the power and designer any more. You just marvel and experience Spirit.

Sometimes the breaking is painful, but the miracles are worth it and the voice that keeps appearing as

Knower and Witness…as Light, as faith.

Beauty, Donna

So, there is a response to everything, a shredding of fabric before the threshold is revealed. Nodding a yes to the air, affirming what is heard within, acknowledging the voice as constant and true. But it's truly the outer world that mixes the colors, transforms the muck and then highlights the individual pieces of transformation. The inner world of glory and Light holds the wisdom carriers; the rambling lines of Haiku on the nightstand, the faint edge of mystery forming drops of rain at midnight on the windowsill, prophets sealing prayers in jars with jasmine, opening them only when we can bear the messages of surrender...

Beauty, Donna

ometimes it feels like there's a short story in every day.

That the graciousness of the rain washing past me just before I say my final Amen is meant to worship those moments I held in awareness.

The paragraph that woke me up at one a.m. to write in the journal next to my bed.

Capturing the tiny fragments of a dream…and I am awake again.

That a kiss on the cheek from a friend was the sweetest greeting and surely my heart was in fullness for hours on end…

That one could truly fly with the cardinals in the gardens while swinging in the sunset's burning aura.

That story that holds the fiery love still ablaze in the heart where Spirit comes alive.

Watching for the invitation…the avenue…a scattered pathway… a blessing…a ray of Light from beam to beam…and breath to breath.

To gently toss pieces of mystery before my eyes.

My ears to hold the message…

to praise what lies before me…

to bow in Wisdom's ground.

Beauty, Donna

It always comes when the mind is too dull or the garden too dry.

That rhapsody of blue, that sweet ache of a day in August.

Where memory seems to rise, more often than prayers.

And there is a sideways tilt of the head; where we need everything to be straighter or less narrow.

Garden gates swing, children are back in place because it is fall.

And the heart says we are still living with need of water.

Thirst rolls off the heads of babies being baptized and we wonder if we will remember, too.

Or did the night cover the sky for longer than one turn of the moon?

Beauty, Donna

So yesterday I told a story to someone who needed to hear just a tiny bit of truth about her own goodness…There was Grace, sitting at the counter next to us and every time my friend lowered her eyes or reared back her head in unkind comments about herself, I touched my heart and said, "Oh you haven't met my lovely friend Grace yet."

Finally, my friend with the liquid eye liner and the tired eyes threw up her arms and said, "WHAT are you talking about?"

And I took out a small heart shaped rock from my purse that is my constant companion and placed it on the table…I waited…and waited, just seconds you know, but time ticks off and makes one shake a bit in these circumstances. And my friend picked up the heart shaped rock and placed it in her hands and rolled it around a bit…

and a bit more, and I waited and waited some more.

Grace is extremely patient. Grace is kind. Grace doesn't even know what the word judgement means…Grace smiles gently at how hard we are on ourselves…Grace nods often when we talk to her. She has this way of confronting without confusing; with this presence that knows all about the humanness, but mainly the heart and the direction of the mind. She really knows a person well enough to raise the bar, to insist on kindness…to bear witness to the journey of the soul and to reveal the goodness within.

Grace goes with me everywhere. She loves to ride in the car, and oh the plane, she LOVES the plane, and, to meet up at the grocery store, to bend next to me in the gardens…she prays with me in the mornings and knows my muses well…

Beauty, Donna

Be gentle out there—lots of healing going on at this time of the year. Bells are ringing; and people are singing...just be gentle out there. Look to your right, then look to your left...hold onto their hands when crossing the street...Stay in when it's cold and you need to rest; say "I love you" before they leave and shut the front door...Hold open a door, carry something with you that you want to give away, blow kisses to babies as they stroll by ...Be gentle in your heart space. We are going to make it through.

Light a candle for the beauty of the hour. Whisper, "Thank you for the gift," ten times a day until gratitude is breath in and breath out. You will find the heart grows wider and Spirit seems closer. Be gentle out there, a lot of healing going on this time of the year.

Beauty, Donna

oday it's about my friend Ruth. She is actively dying/living with cancer. Ruth reads my stories, so she knows I'm writing of her today. A few weeks ago, we sat on her porch swing before the heat of the day rose, and we talked like women talk and smiled like women smile. We've known each other for seven years now and poetry is where we fell in love with one another's voice and the movement of inner kingdoms.

That glorious rehearsing for another realm speaks of fields and openness. Ruth and I fight battles when we sit on the porch swing. We imagine life lived as she is dying. We spend an hour every day designing places she can go in her mind and setting up fortresses and rearranging furniture, taking down rooms that are too small, widening corridors and adding windows.

One day we found a key to an attic and hid a basket of Almond Joy bars on a shelf, near the photos of her children, near a favorite line from the Psalms: 139…"You have searched me, Lord, and you know me. You know when I sit and when I rise; you perceive my thoughts from afar, before a word is on my tongue you, Lord, know it completely…"

Ruth and I have been sharing stories together every day now because it's almost time to gather and say goodbye…Until we meet again…And we find a new swing and a new line of poetry that speaks of the Beloved… and we fall madly in love again and again…

Beauty, Donna

Seekers, smeekers, what are you chasing after?
Spirit whisks by as sunflowers carry heat in their faces.
Tall and lean in September skies.
Rain washes widows free to dream again.
Wind carries breath through earth's deep roots and fault lines…
Fractures along planes, on surfaces, on faces.
And scavengers scan the skies for smaller meals.

Seekers, smeekers, what are you chasing after?
Glory already knows your name.
Just flee from yourself and veils will fall to the side.
Miracles become mystery, waltzing spins to love.
Gravity blends the mystical
And Eternity stops the clock.

Seekers, smeekers, what are you chasing after?
Secrets bend when you are low enough.
Spirit nods, when union reaches One.

Beauty, Donna

Speak your truth.

Walk into the sunset a bit on fire.

Claim the calamity of our time while in conversation with woods and altars covered with

Candles, peace pipes, stoles of Muslims, Christians and Jews.

Prayer beads and sage burnt to the north and the south, to the east and the west.

Healing swell of salvia stems.

Speak your truth. A bit entangled in a weary world,

While standing tall, not calling it right or wrong.

Find the friendship that you won't break up with.

The beauty you cannot resist.

The transformation that you will surrender to.

The call you will bow to.

The moment you dissolve into the song of the cardinal,

You will be free.

Beauty, Donna

Somewhere along the line, we need to be healers.

That sought-after part of the self that knows it will survive, and brings others along with us.

Some days, I can hardly believe what is asked of us on this planet.

How mourning brings the kingdom between heaven and earth into a state of eternity.

Finding roads overturned and under-walked.

Spirit stretching the limits, finding lanes to ramble down, while stilling the heart so fear will not wander.

There is a sweetness that sets the heart on fire and tastes a bit of glory while we are here.

Shelters hope and spreads an altar before us, like the healers we truly are.

Beauty, Donna

So, I am sitting in the sanctuary of my beautiful church this morning and we are doing the Examen (an ancient meditation of giving and receiving) and I hear these words from a tiny voice in the back of the church.

"One, two, three, four, five, six" and the rustling of crayons and paper. And I think, "God is in the house"…and what has been given has now been received…And the babies cry and the people rise and sing…And my heart fills when I clap my hands and there are rocks and mountains… and angels.

There is a drummer with a beat keeping us all together.

And the bread of life and the wine that runs down my fingers as people dip bread into a cup of blessing with Light flowing through and out and into the world.

There is communion in ways that speak to broken hearts and laughter;

to new life and memories of those we loved deeply;

to touching a new baby girl and there is nothing but tears between mothers, because it is all life.

And it has meaning and through it all…

We are heard and known.

We are the pillars that can crumble and the holiness of temples.

And for that I am grateful.

Beauty, Donna

Oh, most Holy God,

What is it about a Kingdom on Earth that is so glorious? That invites us to partake in the journey with a boldness and a sense of inner freedom? A newness that eliminates separation and brings a sense of wholeness and contentment. The peace that passes all understanding… A jar of fragrance spilling all over the world, down the street, through the neighborhood…A slight scent that would remind us of your constant presence, Lord. The lingering of your Glory as we visit a friend…make a phone call to someone in the hospital…sit around a table with our families. The fragrance of beauty in a November sky, the wonder of colors as the sun begins to rise, the sparkle of light found in the eyes of those we hold dear.

What is it about a Kingdom on earth that is so glorious? A home where we are challenged to live from a deep heart, a generous spirit, a Light that can stand in the darkness and not be afraid. A spark of the Divine walking with our brothers and sisters. Trading stories, healing wounds and forgiving ourselves and others…while learning to praise your Holy Name.

Humble us, oh Lord, so that we might hear your guidance and wisdom… to trust what is so freely given as the gift of life. Help us to reach beyond what we thought we could do…what we believed to be true…for you are always and forever challenging us to see more clearly and to believe that such a love exists. That your Holy Spirit empowers us to live fully.

Raise our hearts, oh Lord, so that they rattle within us for freedom, for justice and mercy…So that the breath within us becomes one with yours. And when we whisper what is on our hearts, you whisper back …

When we bow before you in the quiet of our hearts…we are heard, we are known…we are loved.

Amen

Beauty, Donna

When the Pray-er Becomes Prayer:

It is not unusual for people who are prayers to experience Light…for the evening hour of gratitude to sink deeply into the heart… for the mind to reveal language that the soul has been whispering off and on all day long.

It is not unusual for people to see visions of loved ones passed and to bring their name before the Presence that hears all of one's thoughts… passing through the lining of our hearts…remembering important details that bring a sense of beauty and truth to the sunlight. It's not unusual to die a tiny bit in a given day…so Spirit has room to widen the inner Kingdom…to heal the broken…to claim the glorious life that is being formed one moment at a time…to pronounce the dreams that every heart believes are there…

To close one's eyes into the darkness…fading far enough to dream…to dance in the veils of soul's longing…and when morning shines just close enough to touch a ray passing through the slates in the blinds…there the voice is heard…The softly anchored core of knowing…where answers come before my eyes open full…

It is not unusual to pass an angel presence at the grocery store and inwardly bow. To smile as the peace rises through abandoned spaces empty and dry within the flesh of glory…a temple small and shy.

And grace nods from the corner of my eye and one can only smile…

It is not unusual for women gathering to share that they are courageous warriors, not empty vessels. And I smile with a language there are no words for.

For on those days, every day…there can be colors of wisdom and rhythms of dancing that brings the forgotten realm of Love…home to the heart…

then the pray-er becomes the prayer.

Beauty, Donna

Someone said recently, "All I did was say a little prayer and my life changed." The moon challenges the sun for space in the night sky...Prayers glide along the edges of time and space...Radiant rays of light from windows draped with thin blush colored sheers...A slight turn to the left when the soul begins to stir, and shooting stars drop through shields crackling with a vibration that spins down a corridor where Holy, Holy lives...through bone and flesh...Where dreams sing long before the morning light awakens...

That little prayer that knew not why, or how it came to be...but had the power to seep through veils, to step into the moment of light and life... was bigger than was known...For every heart has a fine road to travel... something rising within...a breath caught in the lining of the heart... some wisdom to bestow...

There really is no such thing as a little prayer...For everything is known in the creation of the Soul...the shades of tiny leaves...words one heart knows but we call a thought or dream. The short distance between a whispered pain, a dangerous tug, a blink from what was to what is...The answers before one's eyes are fully waking, then the words begin to fall from higher and higher...to the ground...

Beauty, Donna

A tiny sparrow continues to sit atop the bright red hummingbird feeder during the day. He seems to be drawn to the color, or is just missing the blue birdfeeder not more than fifteen feet away. Perhaps a slight turn in his view and he could see it. But aw, the passion of red and the way he tries to adjust his weight on the foot piece, meant for something so much smaller.

He doesn't stay long, yet morning prayer and writing time seem to always coincide and we are together for seconds And that is all it takes to feel the heart expand and for the mind to take a turn. Some new direction of inspiration or release. A dialogue between, a relationship with, the opening to that world of in and between that we each belong to.

Feathers and a wing. Human with a God.

His eyes dart to mine and I forget the color of his beak or the way his head tilts to the side. The electricity snaps into place; the startled reaction of two becoming one. Sleep from the night still present and a warm blanket on the lap.

There comes a time when two worlds align and though we talk of inner and outer, the thread grows tighter and tighter in the fabric of soul…

A feather and a wing and a human with a God are all the same…

Beauty, Donna

Winter

Mayberry Street is quiet these days. Frosted streets and slippery ice patches that a few dog walkers watch for. January, the month of God's sleep and winter slumber. Lamplights still on when I awaken to do morning prayers and light candles at the cottage.

Something slows, though Spirit waits for its next move...of energy or hope...of witnessing, of moon. Some signs of distance between what actualizes as responsible spiritual growth, and the longing for blankets to keep one safe and warm...That chord of tension, placed in the body... leaving the garden and heading for responsible action in the world.

And Carl Jung would have us actualizing...adding mandalas to a second *Red Book**...Or Thomas Merton would have us place hope in the center of relationships and renewal...Worlds of Hindu mystics read as present day and instruments of universal laws. Way deep down inside us...one God wrapped in reverence and revelation for a time and a place that is held in immense grace.

God witnessed as flashes of lightning and glimpses of deeper dust...It's amazing what you can't say when Spirit lives within you...and waves of words that do not have form

Yet, open and transcending . Lifting the thoughts and the edges of human consciousness opening the door to the next realm.

We've barely moved mountains, and yet Light is lit and the rights of passage are before us.

One day and this alone is all we are given...

Be gracious and kind...Be courageous and weak...humble and wise. Be of good health and care for those you love...It's such a tiny thing... sewing with thread and mending the tear...

Beauty, Donna

*The Red Book by C.G. Jung

Hope and the Healers:

The first sermon I ever wrote was called Beauty and the Helpers. Today, it's Hope and the Healers. I don't know if anyone will ever hear it...truly hear it unless you drop inside to the place of the Holy of Holies...But the words are on paper and the channel was set to, on, when it came pouring out onto the pages. Fingers couldn't stop typing to correct the typos, nor find paragraphs, the beginnings and then the end. It just spoke, all by itself...like that swirl of wind blowing off the crusted red Japanese maple leaves.

A day in January when frost was still thin on the ground, and the white coat of my Great Pyrenees was a blur out my side vision. His seven months of energy bounding through the gardens, snapping the frozen tops off the sedum still standing as property guards. A season of sweetness and healing.

The turning of a pendulum that only happens every eight years; and I don't know if that's symbolic rhythm to people falling off horses, being blinded by Light, or whether it's the timing of the world and eternity breaking in.

Places with clocks, where winter can only quiet with storms and softly fallen snow. Pastel quilts with threads of silken golds and greens.

We need Hope and the Healers.

And on a day when communities gather and church bells ring; or perhaps it's seeing the mountain top for the first time, or sliding through a passageway that finally has a door.

Being known by the Divine, deeply heard and treasured seems like the greatest hope there is.

Beauty, Donna

There comes the day, when you move on…And Joni Mitchell's "Clouds" keeps the rhythm and harmony going in one direction…"I've looked at clouds from both sides now…from give and take and still somehow…"

Waking from a dream or stirring in the clouds, the illusions seem to come less frequently and food for thought is more about the bridge between realms and the eternity in the ordinary day.

I still miss taps and Spirit wisdom but it's not from lack of trying…But because I love the Mystery. Being surrounded with bites to swallow sometimes takes the digestive system a bit longer to process and for the balm of clarity to seep through the layers.

Preaching has never looked so inviting…nor the world at large…or the way Spirit touches the sore spots and heals the memory. How gifted each soul is; and how far some have traveled to experience this type of miraculous energy bound in pure love.

Looking through a glass dimly lit is like inching your way through a narrow tunnel.

Every thought counts when you are transforming…Every angle that you can turn influences the shift in higher consciousness. Every breath that mingles near the edge of wonder and faithfulness rides longer and deeper than any other form of mind chatter.

Every deed matters…the smaller, the better…Each deed is richness far beyond stored jewels in a box on the bedroom dresser. Piercing beauty that can never be held, but flows effortlessly through the body.

Every word spoken shifts the alignment. There is power in holy words that transcend and renew.

Offering the cup of blessing and the vision of a veil removed from one's eyes. It isn't far from the truth though I am an imaginative sort…

To dream into peace is a practice that comes from the ancient ones. But then, soul has been swirling around and within for thousands of years, capturing what it looks like and feels like to be human and bound to choices within the Mystery of miracles and mayhem.

Beauty, Donna

So, at the end of the day…it is cold and tender in Nebraska… Things only mothers understand…about birthing and babies… about drawing lines in the snow and putting carrot noses on snowmen…

How communion breaks and bread is torn.

How loneliness is fed; and Mystery is blown through open windows.

And veils dropped from this side of the moon…

while on the other side…

there are constellations and a Big Dipper.

Moms rocking sleepy heads to sleep while humming the prayer of St. Francis.

How many lullabies the world could use this night…

Waking under a December lamplight…

Rabbit footprints in the snow and three candles lit this night…

When we reach the eve of waking…finding balance in the bushes and the trees…lighting campfires for the water and the air…

Crones circle and women bow their heads…

Beauty, Donna

Prayers for the Journey

My go-to words when I'm reaching for holy buoyancy. I say it a lot. When someone dies, when someone is in rehab, and when everything seems like a continuous movement of change and expectation. I'm not the person you should ask to write or speak on prayer, as it is my lifeline and there are a thousand ways to bow...to kiss...to twirl...to sacrifice...to mingle with the mailman when he says his wife is in the hospital...And out of the depths comes, "prayers for the journey," and a bow of adoration.

Adoration for the beauty of the gift that has been given. So, in this realm, joys and sorrows often meet at some diner in Dundee or when I'm walking the dogs. Or even while rocking my grandson or playing in a sink of water that holds dinosaurs and the laughter of small children.

I have never been successful at separating life experiences into left, but not right or I'll just take this corner of the piece of pie but never enjoy the whipped cream on top.

My prayers go deeper and my heart breaks more often. I wrestle and bow at the same time while writing notes in cards that carry little stone hearts and speak to hope and beauty. But, I still write the words, "prayers for the journey," though it may seem an uninteresting companion.

But, truly, every experience with Spirit is a holy one and holy seeps way down deep into your toes, and rattles around in your gut. Sometimes it explodes out your sides and frightens the people sitting next to you. Or it gurgles in your belly until you hear the heart cracking, just around the edges.

We heal open...We heal with our palms up..

We heal because we whisper things to God while buying groceries and standing in line; we utter words that have been threaded through time and space for this moment and this day.

We say "prayers for the journey" while trusting that all is sacred and holy...And we are known by our name and the beat of our hearts...

Beauty, Donna

If I Stop Praying

If I stop praying, I'll lie down and rest too long. I'll want to sleep instead of rising to the colors of a new day and the simple task of gratitude is my biggest act of surrender.

I'll stop listening. I'll forget how to bow in humility, how to fumble in weakness and where my strength comes from.

If I stop praying, I'll think it's just me in the world, alone and in madness, instead of in the community of others. I'll forget to dance wildly.

If I stop praying the realm of glory that I've been formed in, I will lead to disbanding what has brought me into harmony with my sisters and brothers… with the consciousness of compassion and freedom.

I pray day in and day out. Spirit holding ground beneath my feet.

Spirit pressing on the muscles of my heart, circling round and round where peace has bent so low there is no division between my life and yours. I pray because there is wisdom to be heard and honored.

I pray, because I'm not afraid

to stand

to shelter

to walk beside

to lean against,

to die for another.

To believe it is possible,

to open my arms,

to break with my heart.

To sing while I cry,

to lead while I stand.

Beauty, Donna

She underlines the sentence that grabs her attention in paper #4, assignments to complete a call.

"Spirit pulling from each of us, the gifts that light up the world."

And I wonder if she knows, even after she writes the word, "lovely" with an exclamation mark.

I want the words to flow easily so all can hear. Jesus says one thing, but so does a poem. What lies within me, lies within you.

She says it is like a prose piece and rather lyrical...And I imagine Jesus, too, perhaps had rhythms to speaking of God who designs inside the heart. And if Thomas Aquinas says, "We are all madly in love with the same God," then it is saintly, therefore true...And something within us is seeking harmony.

As above, so below, I see me, I see you...There is no line that divides you, or heightens me.

I know I can carry you on my back and we can bridge the gap...There is a rising and descending. We will find plateaus to rest; we will spread a table on the rocks. An offering of bread and a cup of blessing for the road. And we say prayers for the journey, in your tongue and mine.

Jesus and poetry. We are each emptying and filling, the Kingdom within...

Beauty, Donna

As the crow flies," really needs to fall under a Zen koan or a Jesus parable. Finding the shortest distance between two points has not always been the easiest of things; and digging down deeper into our humanness is somewhat of a fascinating sidecar adventure. When I intuitively follow my spirit nudges and whispers, there is actually a trajectory that appears. Straight and on course, rarely…

But I still see a curve up ahead or recognize the way the branches sway in the woods where I walk. And even now, being here in this place of ancient Native American sky and tepees circled in encampment, there is something that I recognize and speak within myself. And the craving of that stillness, where everything is spoken, and the craving of slipping through the widened door to the next threshold, is forever beating within me.

Or at least whispered from behind the back, or around the trunk of a tree, a childhood game of hide and seek and the possibility of understanding another language pops through the cloud of unknowing.

And where we were moments ago is in the past. Here with beauty singing to the soul, God is standing.

It took so long to get here, and then it was time to not look back, ever again,

Just this one day given…

Beauty, Donna

I took just one little prayer to bed with me last night.
It had been walking around with me for days…

I could hear its whispers, feel the nudges pressing against my heart. I heard the sighs and restlessness as I entered Walgreens yesterday afternoon for Ghirardelli chocolates, the mint ones, that mom loves to keep in the bowl of her tiny kitchen, at Bethany Retirement Living up north.

I found the aisle with the fluffy red socks and the green ones with the reindeer on the toes and threw them in my basket. Thin feet need fluff in the cold nights of the Midwest; and Mom would delight in the characters of Christmas and the memories it brings.

Pockets of prayer words came as I checked out in the fast lane and as I walked to the car in the frigid winds, shawl covering my nose and asthmatic lungs, the Presence I've known for so long descended.

Down into my gut where pushing things away will only prolong the work. Down into the swirl of matter and spirit where holy light had been made manifest. Down through the contemplative cells and the flames of conscious rising, where beads of attention and awareness had been strung together with years of passionate work.

I stopped earlier to do my quiet time of prayer in the sanctuary… Already placed the candles in the kitchen and written three blessings for the day in December that had brought such joy to my heart. I already witnessed miracles of love and sung praises of adoration in my heart…But this seemed so very hard…And the moment of surrender was so close, it was painful…

I know the patterns and the rhythms to my resistant, to identifying my fears and my longings…Quotes of Carl Jung, poems by Rumi, prayers of other faiths that have shattered greater illusions…And yet when it comes to those moments of bending so low, I dissolve into grace and the peace that passes all understanding…

I go limp with the desire to be closer to God…for the many mountain tops to come down into the valleys and to stand next to me…For in all reality, for this realm, we are closer this day than we will ever be…So in the aisles of Walgreens and in the days before, these words of Spirit carried such a passion to be known by me that I had to listen…had to shut out the ways I work with ritual and wonder until I could hear the deeper prayer that was pestering me…

So last night just as I was ready to shut off the night light, I closed my eyes once more and heard.

Be patient with the world...I AM here...

Beauty, Donna

And in the morning when I rise, there's been a softening and a respite...Evening prayers answered in thoughts that are now safe and held lightly...Frozen earth but softened vision, harsh to the lungs and the skin in the cold...But gentle to the care of the world and beloveds. It takes a lifetime...every season turning around the sun,

every moon phase a symbolic gesture that leads to a healing...A window of possibility or even, a chance for a breath...

A friend said to me recently, "I'm not so bothered by the fluff this year, there are more important things." And I nodded...wrapping my mind around her words and hugging the wisdom of her mood.

Creating something real takes greater courage and radical transformation.

Sometimes it's slippered steps to put a note of "how are you doing this day" into the mailbox. And other days, fully a movement of grace to step out and into the complexity of how hearts can open one moment and close the next...How tall people can reach to the top shelf of the grocery store and hand you down the last jar of strawberry jam, but shorter people read what's right in front of them and spill out the news.

Vulnerability speaks to paradox and illumination takes care of the rest...Whether wandering by stars to find a way through or diving through waves to get to the depth and the stillness...We are humans drawn to know what lies beyond fences, broken mirrors and passageways of perception...

Beauty, Donna

We are such extremists,

it's a good thing,

there's the moon.

A gigantic ocean of beauty in the sky.

The waning of tides and a shore. Something to draw emotions to the center…to prick the tip of a finger, or drain a jar of water over dried marigolds.

I have given way to wandering through just as many weeds, as the beauty of the fields…Just as many tears as the waves of peace that passes through flesh and bone on a given day. As many breaths counted to still…as the one lone sparrow cheeping outside the bedroom window.

I could borrow from poetry and lines of Wisdom…the talents of scripture.

But the unfolding of beauty seems to be the one that never dismisses a thing…

Beauty, Donna

In the winter months of Mayberry Street the icy streets slow walking down, but the movement of God never ceases. Even as my neighbor drops off her yearly Christmas goodie bags with homemade fudge and crackers with herbs and seasonings to top hot soup on a snowy day.

Mayberry Street sees through the closed doors and the slower pace to the generosity of hearts and physical bodies shoveling snow for neighbors, or salting sidewalks for dog walkers going by.

Even from the inside the little yellow cottage, where the heat comes up through the wooden vents and the crockpot is steaming with barbeque chicken for the evening meal, Spirit moves within the silence of snow and the menagerie of flock gathered at the cobalt blue bird feeder near the stone wall surrounding the front yard. It's subtle…so, very subtle. This God of heart and spirit of kindness moves the general stranger to go forth and to give just a tiny bit of something extra to another, when it's so very cold, and we need warmth.

How often I think of my friend Anne from earlier days of seminary and her lovely partner who recently passed away. How holidays are different when things change and we are in the daily reminders of what was and what is now gone.

Forms changing forms and holy gifts in new form and creation.

Something has left; but something new is being created. And so it is. And so it goes. And we are asked to become something new, that never has been before. We are asked often to shift into new beings and to carry that wisdom forward.

Over and over again I find on Mayberry Street, the God of beauty and hope revealed and resilient.

Beauty, Donna

You can feel it like rain

Pattering outside your windowpane.

As the snow melts, and the earth soaks up.

You can hear it, like my grandma's arms,

The tree swing in the backyard when I was a child.

The way walking with dogs feels like an intimate adventure

That only fur and human will remember, and soul knows soul.

You can hear it in the kitchen when the oven warms—up,

When the kids pop over to drop something off,

When it's Thursday at the grocery store and all the elderly gentlemen

Are waiting for the ladies to get off the van to help them with their carts.

You can hear it under trees, wading in the foam by the ocean,

Visiting a junk store with boxes of old photos

that look like they came from your tribe,

But they didn't.

You can hear it when you enter a cathedral,

Where the silence brings a bow.

Something borrowed from another time

That lives within the soul.

Walks on the earth.

Witnessing life in the now.

Beauty, Donna

Spring

It feels like forever. The slow yawn of awakening. Weeping while waiting. Holding ground, upon ground, upon ground. Earth heaving with sighs. Some come. Shaken and wondering about this God, a Lord.

Angel passageway. Healing bones and bodies.

Scooping out—

A phrase that bewilders some, frightens others. Fear again. That space in the mind that tolerates all the voices, and yet, it's time it is left behind.

Teaching, they come. Student, prophet, saint and fallen witnesses. Standing, Spirit rises in physical form. Seen, known, revealed.

Sinners—forgotten how to love. Spirit easing the turn, reversing the end to beginning.

Shallow lands, yet deep waters. Drowning. Safety. Collapsing inward, surrendering, breath in and breath out. Diaphragm expanding through blood and forgiveness.

Profound. Emptying. Miracles defining space and time, true knowledge shifting perception.

Sampling …tasting, touching, sensing, seeing, hearing how to love in a world of sleeping souls.

Just mirror back what student, prophet, saint and fallen witnesses know. Spirit rising in physical form.

It is not the anger of the past we see; it is the fear of falling in love with the present.

The healing work, the stillness mirroring back…invisible gods in corners of rooms, entering into communion. Setting reality where it belongs.

Beauty, Donna

The sun rose just as prayers began with an obsessive love for the earth.

A thirst for the rains to seep further down to the roots;

Same in my soul.

The adoration that sits at the edge of a new day; and breath is simple and low.

The endless practice of breath in and breath out.

Where stillness joins three inches of tulip leaves pushing through the ground.

And revelation and prayer are one.

The sun rose just as prayers began.

The fever of love and glory rising.

Beauty, Donna

PRAYERS FOR THE JOURNEY...that's what I've got...

Sometimes no one wants to hear "prayers for the journey" because a journey is a lifetime...And change, grief and transformation is a process...

I post on other sites...It doesn't end with a sigh in the heart, a card to a friend, a blessing on their day...prayers for the journey is for a lifetime of day in and day out...The times when the memories come back, are triggered, someone says the "wrong" thing and the pain pockets erupt into memory...Prayers for the journey.

Someone once said to me "I don't want it to be a journey!" and I know what she means. But, after living 58 years and Spirit radically altering my vision of life and death here...I still pray the most dangerous prayers that will shift and shatter what veils hide from reality, from consciously growing...life long process...with much help and guidance along the way.

So, when the gift is given...prayers for the journey.

I send you love, radical amazement as to where you'll be three months from now.

The gift of hope and in siding you out...For Spirit rides the wind in mysterious ways...And all prayers are heard and all prayers are answered.

Beauty, Donna

A Reflection on Psalm 119

What joy is Your Holy Mystery that fills these days. To be bathed in the sacredness of all things visible and invisible.

It was the exquisite risk you drew me to…the wild abandonment that left me weak…to let go…leaning into all that I could have of you.

You were my piercing prayer…a path lush and green…a heart that walked the edge of a stream hearing nothing but woodland trees and a call that pulled me through the walls into Light…And I would turn and greet angels walking side by side…

You taught me to trust the swallowing up with the darkness and the flicker of a candle light consuming all, until the fragrance and sweetness spilled over onto my skin.

Oh, the splendor and freedom…I fall and run…drawing on the walls… colored chalk smeared on my hands.

Surely sunlight draws radiance to the shadowed halls.

You unfold before me.

Flowers in vases and rock on the ground.

Wisdom shown as wonder,

raspberry clouds and humus body drawn to the ground.

What joy is Your Holy Mystery that fills these days,

a promise and a vow.

Lessons learned by sun and moon, stories of Your truth…a veiled road to follow.

"Breathe," you said, and with a final act of surrender, there burst within me thresholds that knew my name.

What rises from you, gives birth within me. Delighted to be born—and I bow.

Beauty, Donna

It was an ordinary day, and God came to watch the thunder and the lightning…

near my side…

It was at the edge of the garden bed, just as the clouds began to open and the gate through the fence had been left wide.

That presence of power and glory slipped into the humid air and I paused, deep breath in, deep breath out. I paused with that slight awareness of being together, and among, and within the glory of something beyond this time and space. It's so subtle and moving slowly, as the line sung from a favorite tune that you've always known.

Beauty, Donna

Remember that people wake up in different times, zones, heights and depths.

One may be in the winter of their spring.

While another in the dark night of summer or visiting the hot springs of Arizona.

Remember that people wake up to different sounds and harmonies,

Different from your own.

That the singing bowl on the counter vibrates at just the right

note for soul to respond if you are listening, if it's winter, or perhaps,

when the cat sits on your lap

or someone knocks at the door,

dropping off a Peace Lily that the church had in memory of someone special to you.

Greening is an individual seed,

A single swipe of the sword

Piercing of the Holy Spirit at just the right moment of heart, mind, body and soul.

Remember that timing is of the Spirit; and wisdom takes a long time to grow into the crown of the head.

The patience of God amongst us and God for us.

Faithfulness to a people in different times and differing paths.

Beauty, Donna

I want to know this dream you carry through me,

Of roses, coral and peach stained near the back fence in the gardens, another row of scarlet velvet leaves fallen near a bed of spring dried iris,

of tiny thorns placed within the beauty of a field, visions of beyond a time and place.

I want to know this dream you carry through me,

Rain beating onto skin, aged and lit from within,

Thin and fine near the bone, and Glory builds clay pots from Earth.

Then pebbles of sand…where friends die and all I can hear is,

Hallowed Be Thy Name,

while scattering seeds in empty spaces,

while bowing to the Light within…bearing witness to what rises,

tracing shadows with my fingers.

I want to know this dream you carry through me

while whispering, "Prayers for the Journey," just one more time. A vision of beyond, a time and place.

Beauty, Donna

It has been forty years now since I started writing love letters.

Little squiggles of messy handwriting on pages with flowers.

Some with purple ink on an artist's card with a woman saturated in holy light.

And the card just the right 4 x 6, to hold the number of words that say,

"Holding you close in my heart" or

"Spring will be here soon."

Praying for ease of heart and mind as your body releases and heals.

So very happy the baby has arrived and all is well.

Yes, chicken soup is good for so many things that ail us as well as sitting in the sun when it's that damp kind of rain and your toes won't warm up.

Blessings on your new home and hope the kids like their new school and friends.

And, "When are we having tea and mini cinnamon rolls in the garden next?"

I love paper and pages that turn. Something one can hold in the hand,

Running fingers across the ink to see if it's wet or sun dried,

Right off the black writing desk and slid into a lilac colored envelope.

A stamp of some bird, or a flower or dog.

It looks beautiful and that makes all the difference to the healer of the heart.

Beauty, Donna

100 Miles in Lent:

I completely lost my heart when it first began to happen, many years ago now. Hearing beauty, when others could only hear darkness. Seeing beauty, while the world erupted into chaos and an odd proportion of "out of time and place." Sensing beauty when someone was angry or upset, as I listened to spirit shift the mind, and the heart was filled with this tremendous amount of light and wonder. A radiance that brings deep peace and gratitude…praise and adoration. In a time where beauty brings us into temples, mosques and sanctuaries. While turning and responding to the movement of spirit, there, is Wisdom weaving…

Beauty gathers the heart and unites with something the prophets nor mystics could ever put into words, though they try.

There is that delicious gift one can sense in this lifetime.

Being in the world but not of the world.

Somehow knowing we are known takes the fear out of the ordinary and standing so tall and straight, no matter how strong the winds of March, there is no faint of heart unless a tiny woodland flower rises through the dampened floor and then one could only utter, Glory.

Daffodils come up in the spring, while Light sits at the core of all existence.

Beauty, Donna

So, at the end of the day, worship was about a cup of blessing and wine dripping through my fingers. Serving in the greatest of joy, while blessing the eyes that met mine. Walking a hundred miles, while juggling seminary books, a deck of Beauty coming forth…A whiff of something coming into new shape and form…Sun touching the back of my neck, while climbing ridges I thought not possible yet, but truly more than possible.

Spirit knows the heart, the mind…and configures how to bend an ear to whisper love songs, to entice the Mystery to unfold; Spirit lacks nothing in its attempts to grow a soul, to bandage a wound, to throw out a challenge, or to uplift the heart.

So, at the end of the day, the heart is full, the cottage quiet and filled with a peace that comes from entering into the world. Engaging the stream to flow into the river; bobbing on the ripples when necessary, or diving through the layers…

Praying words while passing strangers, blowing kisses to babies in strollers, and dancing with anyone who will shuffle just a bit to the right in the grocery aisle so I can reach to the top shelf…Humans touching humans in the language of love.

Tearing off a piece of bread and dipping it in the cup of blessing.

How sweet to feel wine running down one's fingers and to be blessed by the thirst of God.

To take it out into the world where groceries are also dipped in wine, and dinner with family,

love seeping through.

Beauty, Donna

When you see the beautiful,
      it integrates the worlds,
stimulates the mind, and
saturates the body with healing peace.
The beautiful sets a tone for how you live.

Beauty, Donna

Where are the multitudes who love Wisdom?

April skies are stained with burgundy clouds.

Robins sing outside the bedroom window during early mornings.

Memory is caught between the worlds of healing a planet and

Watering the rose bushes.

Tending to those in grief and holding my grandson's hand.

She is the Oneness of all Being.

She is the protector of the interior world and bends deeply,

Listening to the awakening soul,

Somehow young, while very old.

To love Wisdom takes time.

A lingering apart from the day,

While fashioning braids and ribbons into prayer beads that one can count late into the night.

How many pearls slide through one's fingers while saying, "Thy Will Be Done."

And the moon rises outside

Amongst the sixty-foot pines

While Wisdom ripens.

Beauty, Donna

It is good to be holy. To walk a hundred miles without giving or taking, but just walking.

To stand in the woods at the center of a grove of white pines and say nothing at all.

To find space where community is taller than you are and boughs rise to heights you will never reach, or maybe you will.

It is good to be holy. To walk a hundred miles, dropping anxiety, needing forgiveness; melting into emptiness, lowering one's head. Weaving right, then left as the damp earth, pelted with rain, then frozen with ice, draws one deeper into the forest.

It is good to be holy. To walk a hundred miles reciting Rumi, memorized from years of fiery flames and Meister Eckhart's vision that finally became Home.

It is good to be holy. To know inquiry sets the feet on a worthy path.

That Light is more than a lamp unto my feet, but the life lived of the Holy.

Beauty, Donna

Once you have rid yourself, emptied,
Then you wait.

Clean the house, water the plants, push the stroller in the sunshine.

Visit a friend at the hospital, buy groceries, make a phone call to your mother.

Keep listening; it will come.

Once you have rid yourself, emptied, bone dry.

Then you wait.

You watch birds drop down from the sky, picking up scattered seed under the birdfeeder,

Under the heart

Near the ground.

Where lying face flat seems to be reminiscent of slipping through clouds as children gaze on hot summer afternoons, while mothers hand out popsicles through the back screen door.

Bone dry, yet, someone standing near to quench the thirst.

Mothers, like gods, and cousins reaching for cherry flavors,

Dripping sweetness and sticking to everything.

Once you have rid yourself, emptied

Then you wait.

Keep listening, it will come.

Beauty, Donna

We are not really ever separate from anything.

What's broken in the heart is broken in the mind. What's healed in the mind, is healed in the heart.

While held within the body. Framed by bone and a bit of clay spit from the Creator's breath…as a sigh…a longing to be known.

What is read as Parables, is also known as Wisdom literature…is read as Zen koans, is read as Carl Jung;

The mystics experience of intimate knowing of God.

Of awakening to a reality so miraculous that you'd die over and over again to be closer and closer to that love…to that revelation.

Is also heard as ancient and worn through time…Experienced only by those who surrender, who wander and waver…Who are fragile, who are vulnerable to the sought after capturing of Spirit's fire…Who sense something beyond this time and space and glean drops of blood from following the path…around a corner to a new country…

Children wave to angels telling them stories before bed,

and parents say it's make believe…forgetting where dreams take grownups…through the looking glass and into a world with a new lens.

We are not really ever separate from anything.

Not God or wisdom…divine intervention or standing in the rain on a cold day in February…

A few words were spoken before I was born…

and then the beauty began…

Something opening …some would say the psyche begins to play a game and we sideways fall into a new realm of idealism. Or we begin to read paradoxes as daily understanding of the lessons that inspire and inform our path.

Some would just say we begin to awaken and the seasons become fresh with each turning of calendar pages.

Because sometimes we have to remember time and schedules…even within heaven on earth…

Beauty, Donna

You never get to keep the Light, but somehow it circles in all through the day,

Letting it slide through your fingers on a communion Sunday.

The flow of Mystery sets portals on fire.

The insistence of giving it all away, of releasing the lens, in which Spirit has demanded such attention for so long. Then the offering, out into the world; the emptying.

Like a well, being drawn deeper and deeper into the regions of wisdom, humility, and courage. The beauty of profound universal love and connection.

The distance, so near, the whispers can be heard.

The offerings being pulled up, as cord tied to a memory.

We step in. Then we step out, some kind of rhythm knitting the longing.

The needles click together as a shawl becomes web,

And the Light spreads beyond who I am.

Beauty, Donna

About the Author

Reverend Donna is an Interfaith Minister serving individuals and families who seek spiritual growth and guidance in all areas of their lives. She seeks to have her words reach far and wide, to lift up those who are in pain, and inspire those who wish to find their purpose.

Rev. Donna is a Spiritual Director and leads retreats on spiritual writing, grief, wisdom and how gratitude changes your inner lens.

Donna is a graduate of the Mystic Heart Wisdom School in San Antonio, Texas.

She is known as a Poet Preacher and leads workshops on poetry as "The Inward Journey."

She finds joy in traveling, photography, tending her vast gardens, writing, and playing with her grandchildren.

Rev. Donna is a prayer walker and has walked countless miles in preparation for her walking the El Camino de Santiago in Spain in July 2018.

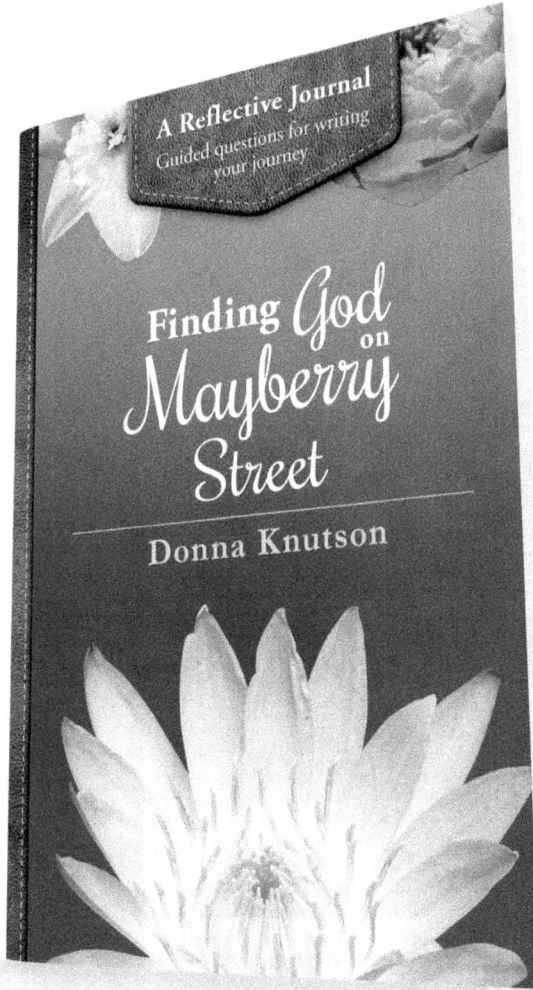

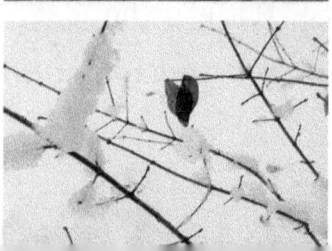

Journal

Where did you see beauty today?

_____
_____
_____
_____
_____
_____
_____
_____
_____
_____
_____
_____
_____
_____
_____
_____
_____
_____
_____
_____
_____
_____
_____
_____
_____
_____

Finding God on Mayberry Street

How did you experience the Holy today?

_____

_____

_____

_____

_____

_____

_____

_____

_____

_____

_____

_____

_____

_____

_____

_____

_____

_____

_____

_____

_____

_____

_____

_____

_____

_____

_____

_____

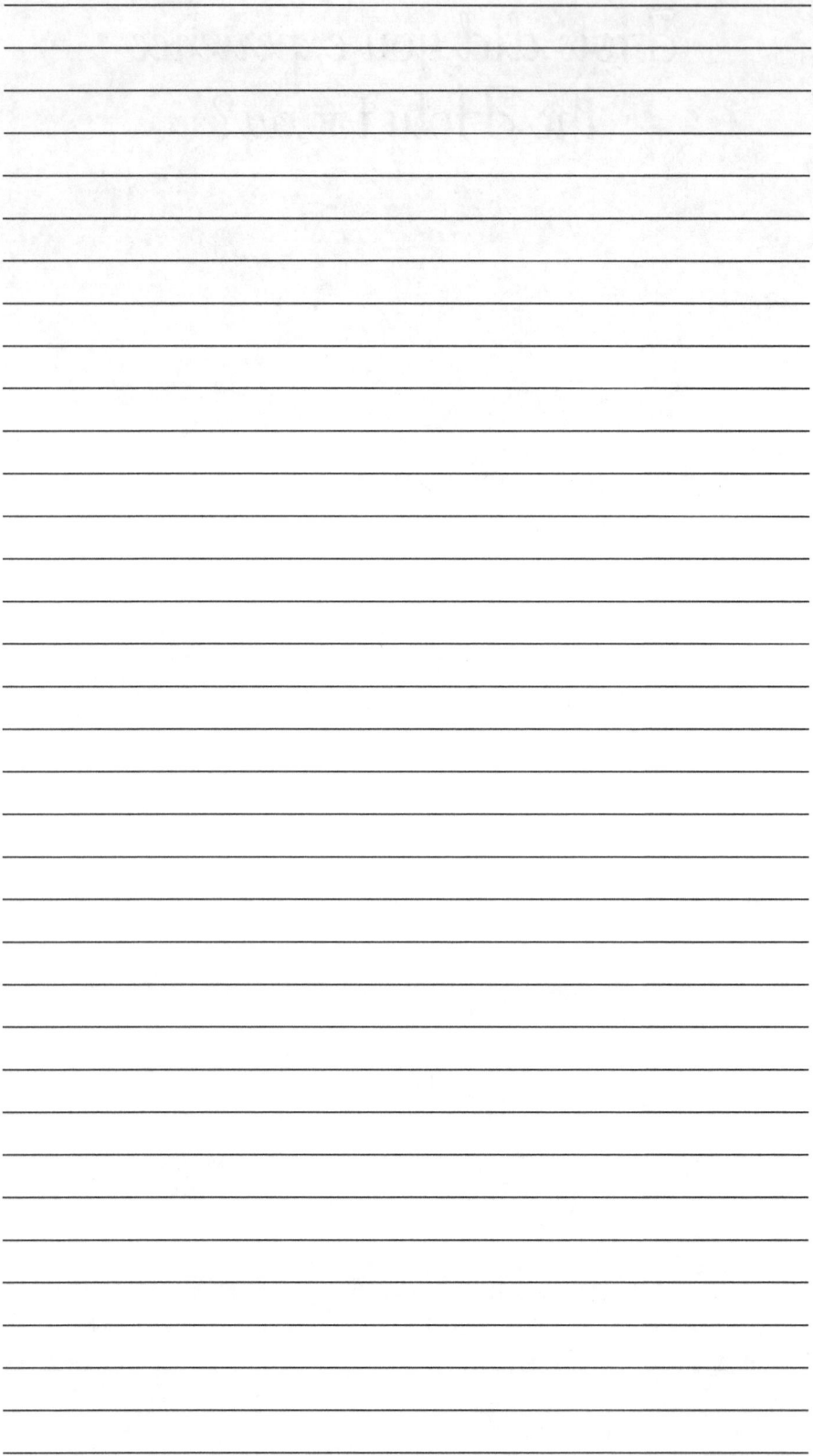

www.ingramcontent.com/pod-product-compliance
Lightning Source LLC
LaVergne TN
LVHW061303060426
835510LV00014B/1852